You might be a turkey hunter if...

You might be a turkey hunter if...

Kenny McDonald

You might be a turkey hunter if…

ISBN: 0-75964-145-5

Cover spread photo by Kathy S. Butt.
Back cover inset photo by DeShae McDonald.
Cover layout/design by Phillip Brackett.
Illustrations by Stephanie Roxas.

1stBooks - rev. 4/23/2001

The idea for this book was sparked in the Spring of 1999 from a thread posted on the turkey hunting talk forum on the huntinfo.com website. Many of the "reasons" were posted on that original thread. In the Spring of 2000, the thread was posted to two additional turkey hunting talk forums - one on tnturkey.com and one on bowsite.com. Permission to use various excerpts from these three threads has been granted by the owners of these websites.

Hunting Information Systems (huntinfo.com) is an on-line guide to hunting-related services and trip planning information for hunting around the world.

TNTurkey.com is dedicated exclusively to Turkey hunting in the "Volunteer State".

Bowsite.com is the largest, fastest growing, and most comprehensive bow hunting website on the internet.

This book is dedicated to all the turkey hunters' spouses who put up with all the crazy antics for about two months out of each and every year.

You might be a turkey hunter if...

You need only 4 hours of sleep during April and May, but need at least 8 the rest of the year.

You see the newest turkey hunting gimmick and your mouth starts to water, your palms start to sweat and you get this vacant look in your eyes with just a little smile on your face!

You finally get a woman to say, "Why don't you give me a call sometime," and you show up on her door step at dawn clucking, purring, and tree yelping until the police arrive.

All the other guys are using pick-up lines in the clubs, and you approach the cutie with a hair-raising gobble.

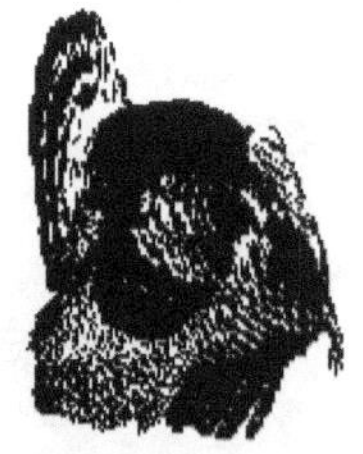

You name your favorite shotgun!

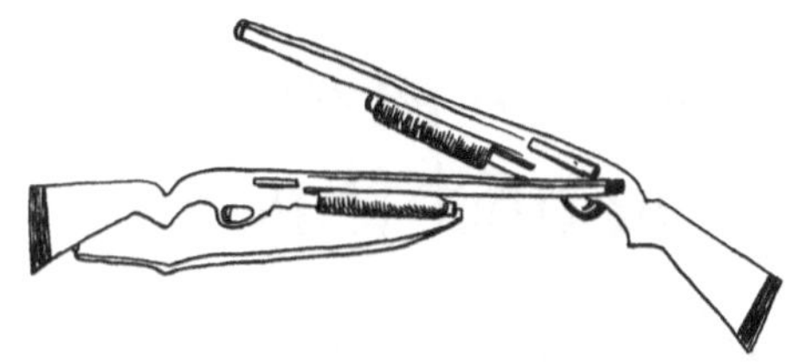

You finally get a woman to say, "Why don't you give me a call sometime," and you hand her a brand new slate/glass double and three exotic laminated wood strikers.

You left your fiancé standing at the alter because the season was extended one day due to bad weather.

You practice on your calling techniques in the hospital delivery room.

The first set of clothes you buy for your newborn is camo pajamas.

You've ever spent hours looking for your favorite striker that was lost somewhere between your truck and your blind.

You name your calls.

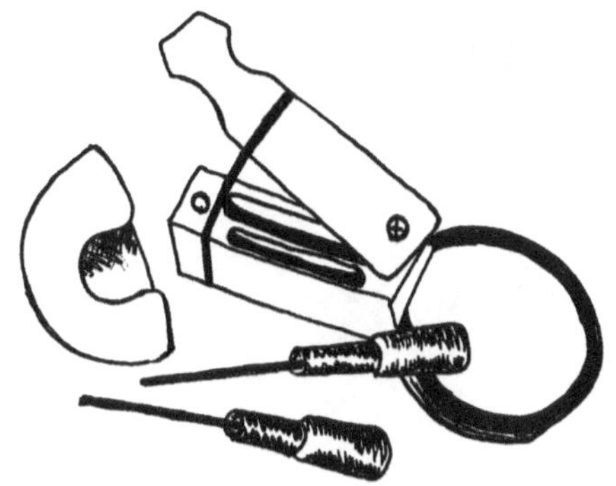

You spend more $$ on a turkey season than you do on your spouse's anniversary present!

You can eat Vienna sausages, or Spam, with your fingers like a starving wolf for about a month and avoid them like the plague the rest of the year!

You know more about a turkey's anatomy than you do your own!

You spend more $$ on a turkey season than you do on your spouse's birthday present!

You are more selective about the type and size of the shotgun shells you shoot than you are about the shoes you wear to church!

You foam at the mouth, lose sleep for weeks, gripe about days passing too slowly and get very interested in a bird's love life every Spring!

You give your new baby a gobble tube instead of a rattle.

You frequent turkey hunting forums on the Internet.

You refer to your spouse as the "Old Boss Hen" or "Old Boss Gobbler".

You're reading this silly book!

You think "gettin' a little tail" is a missed head shot.

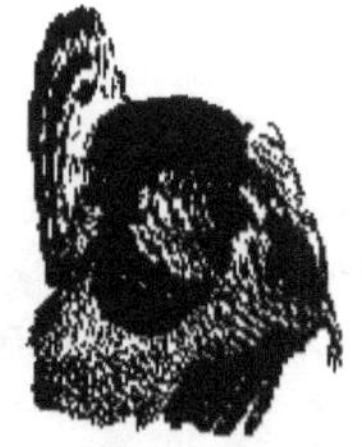

The level of DEET you've absorbed through your skin exceeds EPA toxic waste standards.

Your turkey blind has its own mailbox.

You wake up before the alarm clock goes off for about a month out of the year - without your spouse's nagging!

Your spouse thinks you're doing too much hunting in the woods and not enough hunting in the bedroom.

You get all the dogs
in the neighborhood
torn all to pieces
with your new dog
whistle locator call.

You go to the mall and your better half asks why you keep walking around like you're trying to sneak up on everything.

You get up early every day for weeks before the season opener and sit on the back porch just to listen to them gobble.

Your kids learn to yelp and gobble before they learn to speak.

You've ever changed from your camo into your work clothes while driving down the road.

You know, to the minute, when the sun will come up on opening day of turkey season but forget your anniversary!

You sit in the church pew and remove your hat but put on your camo head net.

You practice with your diaphragm calls on the way to and from work.

You've ever taken out a turkey call and hit a few licks while at work.

You've ever run off the road looking at a flock of turkeys.

You try to make a yelping sound out of anything and everything around the house whose squeak sounds remotely like a yelp.

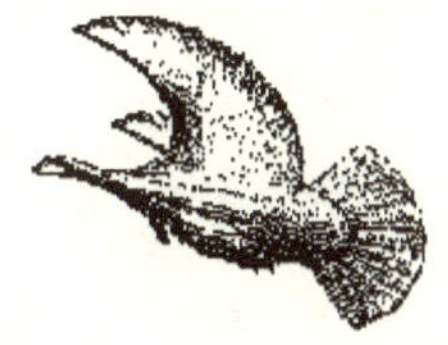

You have one of those "gobbling" alarm clocks.

You carry a turkey call with you everywhere you go - 12 months out of the year.

The hair on your chest has grown out in only one spot and it's 10.5" long.

Your kids know what a "cluck", "yelp", "cutt", or "purr" is - and they know the difference in all of them.

You introduced your wife to the new minister as the "boss hen" and referred to your children as the "poults".

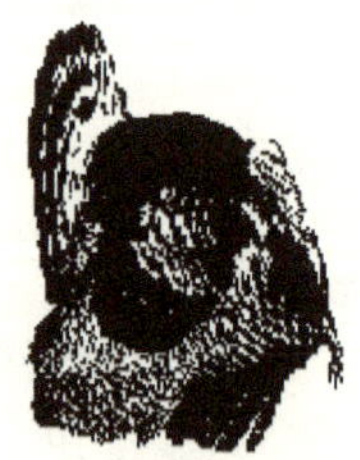

You wear camo undershorts.

Your kids don't know that a cat "purrs" too.

You have absolutely no interest in sex for about 5 or 6 weeks out of the year.

You get REAL TIRED of your co-workers asking "Did you get him yet"?

You named your kids "Jake" and "Jenny".

Your kids run you out of the house playing their music, but you run them out of the house playing with your turkey calls.

You missed your daughter's first dance recital the evening before opening day because you were "puttin' em to bed".

You frequently use terms such as "hung up", "henned up", "limb hanger", "swingin' beard", "full fan", and "runnin' and gunnin' ".

When you watch TV, instead of sitting down in your favorite chair, you roost on the back of it.

When you're glued to this book and the "Old Boss Hen" has to use your favorite slate call to get your attention.

Instead of yawning in
the morning you do
the fly-down cackle.

You have more turkey calls than you can carry, let alone have pockets for.

You become a weather expert the week before the season opener.

You know more about a turkey's sex life than you do your own!

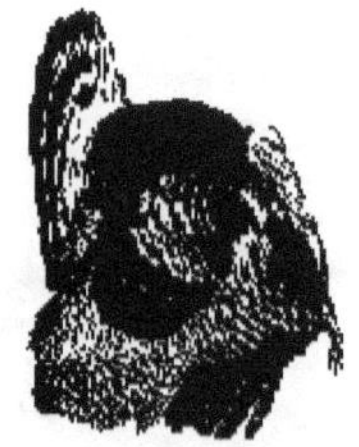

You go to wash your camo, and while dumping out your pockets, all the old turkey turds you picked up fall out.

Your taxidermy bill is bigger than your house payment.

You molt.

You know the pellet count of every turkey shell made, but don't know your kids' ages.

You know the restriction diameter of all the choke tubes available for your favorite shotgun.

You have the "Psychic Turkey Hotline" phone number programmed on your telephone's speed dial.

Your maps and crib notes make your office look like a war room.

You take your turkey foot from last year and put tracks all around an area to throw the other hunters a curve.

You suddenly develop memory loss and become extremely suspicious of anyone asking you, "Well, how'd ya do"?

You make your spouse buy the turkeys for Thanksgiving and Christmas - you CAN'T be seen buying one!

You judge a man's age by the length of his beard.

You have 3 toes.

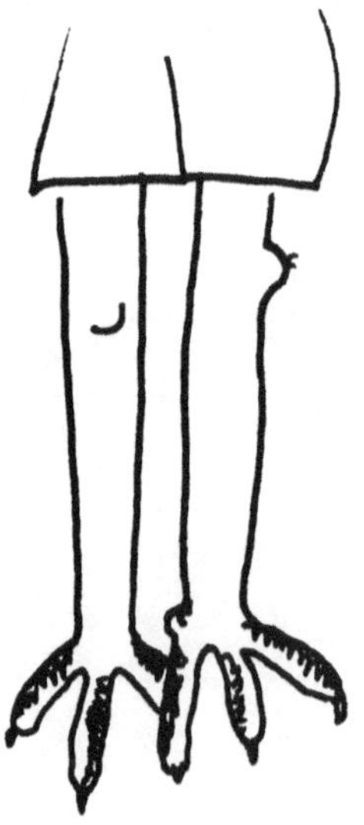

You start to periscope your neck up and down, trying to gain the same advantage the bird has with its vision.

You ask your kids "what sound a turkey makes"? and instead of the usual "gobble-gobble-gobble" you get a half-hearted attempt at a yelp.

You're reading this at work and have no doubt that it IS the most important thing you could be doing with your time.

When you hear a crow in the distance, you immediately become completely still and turn your best ear in the direction of the crow to see if you can pick up a faint gobble!

You try to roost on the bedpost.

You're on your third wife because the last two left to get away from the calling practice in the wee hours of the morning.

You gobble every time your kids slam the truck door.

Every spring you feel an urge to "re-establish the pecking order" in your neighborhood by chasing the mailman and paperboy with your turkey gun.

You and your mate buy your sex toys from your local sporting goods store's hunting department.

You have more camo clothes hanging in your closet than you do dress clothes.

You take longer putting on your makeup than your wife does.

You spend more money on a new set of camo and boots than you did for your last suit and shoes.

You laugh when your hunting buddy talks about your spouse, but poke him in the eye if he talks about your calling skills.

You refer to your bedroom as the "Struttin' Zone".

You let the four deer tags that came with your archery license go to waste trying to fill your two bird tags.

Instead of snoring in your sleep - you "tree yelp".

In the early Spring, you spend more time in the woods scouting than you do at work.

You have a favorite diaphragm call that spends more time in contact with your mouth in a month than your mate does in a year.

You know exactly how many more days it is until the season opener, but don't have a clue how many more days you have to file your income tax return.

Your wife calls you to bed with a diaphragm - a double-reed one that is.

You can sleep while a train rattles by your house 30 yards away, but the drumming of a gobbler 50 yards away wakes you up instantly.

Your email program gobbles at you when you receive new mail.

Your telephone answering machine message consists of your best sequence of yelps, cutts, and purrs, then the words – "That was a good call...Is your's gonna be?".

Your video library is made up entirely of every turkey hunting video ever made.

You can find that roost tree in the pitch black darkness, but can't seem to be able to find that special little store your better half wants to visit at high noon.

You can get up at 4am to get to your favorite hunting spot, but getting up early enough to exercise before work is totally out of the question.

Your house sounds
like a bird sanctuary
each Spring - owls,
crows, peacocks,
hawks, turkeys.

You shock gobble at people when they honk their horn at you.

Starting in February, all conversations somehow refer to turkey hunting no matter what they start out about.

Barred owls roost on your deck because you hoot every evening and every morning.

Your living room looks like a turkey museum.

You have your favorite camo pattern tattooed on your face, arms, and hands.

While looking for your turkey vest and calls, you run across your dusty fishing rods that haven't been touched in years.

Your shotgun shells are colored olive green.

You actually spend more time hunting than you do surfing the Web.

There are three or more diaphragm calls in your cup holder in your truck.

You feel like you need to "strut your stuff" every morning.

The people you work with still can't find where that noise comes from.

Your hunting partner breaks your ribs and saves your life performing the Heimlich maneuver because you swallowed your mouth call.

You can't remember your spouse's cell phone number – but do remember the name and manufacturer of every turkey call you've ever owned.

You run for the house at the first sign of rain while mowing the lawn but will sit through a major thunderstorm if the turkeys are gobbling.

You've ever been reprimanded by your boss because you thought everyone in your plant would enjoy a few yelps, cutts, cackles, and purrs over the PA system.

You might NOT be a turkey hunter if...

You've spent thousands of $$ on hunting equipment and hundreds of hours in the woods and haven't even seen, shot at, or killed a turkey.

Many thanks go out to the following frequenters of the turkey hunting forums on **Huntinfo.com**, **TNturkey.com**, and **Bowsite.com**. Their posts sparked the idea for this book, and they contributed many of the reasons why "you might be a turkey hunter if...".

Wolfman
RayC
Birddog
Chuckhunter
Pygmy
spectr17
Paul in VA
Duster
bamaflier
Greene County Tom
Tom Taker
Ala Jethro
TimberDuck
TPHunter
Smilingg
turkyhntr
hmhunter
DEERDAWG50
shed king
BBS
GobbleStopper
M_R_Dux
HH
Yukon
Bowpredator
HILLBILLY
VolDoug
TNhunter
Southern Sportsman
Turkey Ninja
ctwny1
duffy
rhino99
Strutter
TURK
BUMPER from PA
BBurton
Gadget
Stringpuller
CBennett
PhantomD
TWadlington

Cover photo by Kathy S. Butt, freelance outdoor writer and photographer.

Much of Kathy's wildlife photography can be seen in several major outdoor publications such as *Outdoor Life, Turkey Call, Turkey & Turkey Hunting, Bow & Arrow Hunting*, etc.... Kathy also yearly publishes a ***Focus on Wildlife*** calendar featuring a variety of wildlife photography such as white-tailed deer, wild turkeys, upland game, black bear, waterfowl, and much more.

For more information about Kathy's photography or her ***Focus on Wildlife*** calendars contact:

Kathy S. Butt
Focus on Wildlife
212 Drakewood Dr.
Portland, TN 37148

Telephone # (615) 325-2625

www.ingramcontent.com/pod-product-compliance
Lightning Source LLC
Chambersburg PA
CBHW051441280526
45785CB00003B/1373

* 9 7 8 0 7 5 9 6 4 1 4 5 7 *